We are

MW01697412

many moments of
our lives, and we
are thinking of you
during this difficult
time.

Accept our deepest
love and support

KINCaring

KI family

PS: Let us know if
you need anything

As always, Rabbi Sheryl Lewart has touched our hearts and opened our souls

with the power and beauty of her words. Reading these blessings and meditations are an invitation to enter a spiritual world that links each of us to ages past, stretches our imaginations beyond space and time, and envelopes us in all that is true and essential about life itself. What a fitting testimony to the life she gave so generously to each of us privileged to know her.

Rabbi Steven Carr Reuben, PhD
Senior Rabbi Kehillat Israel Reconstructionist Congregation
Author of a number of books including *Raising Ethical Children*

The harvest of an extraordinary life,

this book is an apothecary for the soul with blessings and meditations to bring healing and peace through the weeks of the years and the days of challenge and celebration.

Rabbi Anne Brener, LCSW
Director of Spiritual Development - Academy for Jewish Religion California

She opens the practice of blessings to all people, not just clergy.

She weaves life's ups and downs into blessings for challenge, for celebration and for comfort. But Sheryl was a Rabbi's Rabbi and she linked each Biblical Torah portion to a unique blessing, a blessing for the journey and that pragmatic chart is portrayed in the book itself.

Rabbi Karen L. Fox MFT
Wilshire Boulevard Temple - Los Angeles, California

This book of blessings
is warm, direct, and accessible –
just what I would have expected from my late and much lamented student Rabbi Sheryl. Read it slowly and savor it; you will find yourself deeply touched as I was by her living presence on every page.

Rabbi Arthur Green
Professor at Hebrew College in Boston
Past Dean (1987-1993) of the Reconstructionist Rabbinical College
Author of *Radical Judaism: Rethinking God and Tradition*

Rabbi Sheryl Lewart has created a brilliant and immediately useful legacy which will endure.
Using the weekly reading of the Old Testament as inspiration, she has created weekly blessings to strengthen, comfort and heal us to find balance, courage and hope. This book is a gift of true companionship. It will surely be used and treasured from adolescence through early, middle and late adulthood and very old age.

Sarah Traister Moskovitz
Professor Emeritas – California State University at Northridge

Rabbi Sheryl Lewart has left us
with a sacred treasure of blessings.
Amidst the sanctity of our past her contemporary style makes it accessible to our everyday life. A profound gift of her soul.

Cantor Chayim Frenkel
Cantor of Kehillat Israel of Pacific Palisades, California

This book was made possible

by the generosity of the friends of

Rabbi Sheryl Lewart.

Blessings for Life's Journey

Transformative Meditations and Readings by

Rabbi Sheryl Lewart

Tambourine Publishing

PACIFIC PALISADES, CA

For information or to order additional copies, contact
Tambourine Publishing
16070 West Sunset Blvd., Suite 106
Pacific Palisades, CA 90272
tambourinepublishing.com

LCCN 2013943130

ISBN 978-0-615-83504-4

Production Management by
Paros Press LLC
1551 Larimer Street, Suite 1301 Denver, CO 80202
303-893-3331 www.parospress.com

Book Design by
Scott Johnson

Printed in the United States of America
First Printing

Table of Contents

Introduction .... *x*
Dedication .... *xiii*
A Blessing Story .... *xiv*
Breath Meditation .... *xx*
A Blessing for Life's Journey .... *xxiv*

Beginnings

Inner Awareness 2
Birth 6
Rebirth 10
Possibilities 14
Transformation 18
Leave 22
Create a Family 26
Journeys 30

Balance

Revelation 36
Perseverance 40
Rest 44
Integrity 48
Balance 52
Cleansing 56
Imperfection 60
Simplify 64
Promises 68
Empowerment 72
Listening 76

Celebrations

Your Birthday 82
Anniversary 83
Yom Kippur 84
Hanukkah 86
Passover 87
Thanksgiving 88

Challenges

Family Relationships 92
Struggle 96
Family Tension 100
Reconcile 104
Freedom 108
Stand Up 112
Resistance 116
Heavy Burdens 120
Doubt 124
Challenges 128
Justice 132
Release 136

Comfort

Healing from Chronic Illness 142
Trust 144
Angels 148
Loneliness 152
Warmth 156
Protection 160

Mistakes 164
Feeling Loved 168
Contentment 172

Heart Songs

Wholeness 178
Intuition 182
Clarity 186
Exuberance 190
Reflection 194
Gratitude 198
Compassion 202
Patience 206
Judgment 210
Courage 214

Loss

Loss 220
The End of Life 224
Grief 228
Acceptance 232
Letting Go 236
Death is Always Personal 240

Blessings for Weekly Torah Portions 243
Acknowledgments 247
Rabbi Sheryl Lewart 249
Psalm 23 - An Interpretation 253

INTRODUCTION

For almost thirty years the blessings found in the Torah have guided, informed and shaped my life. One of the great joys of being a rabbi is to access these life-changing blessings as the Torah unfolds, one narrative after another, one insight leading to the next. Every year, when I return to the reading I read last year, it is different; its effect on my heart is changed because I have changed during the life I've led this past year. Time is not only linear, it swings back upon itself.

Over the past few years, these blessings/meditations were sent to congregants and others who asked to join my blessing list. Each blessing uses the Torah as a touchstone.

This can be your experience as well. By reading these blessings you will be empowered and encouraged to search out what makes each blessing meaningful and helpful to you as you travel your own unique life's journey. Your own journey becomes richer and deeper; insights appear as the Torah offers its thousands of years of wisdom to you in a personal way.

You can access the transformative power of blessings by using the *Blessings for Life's Journey* Table of Contents on page vii. You can use this Table of Contents to select blessings according to your own interests and needs: Beginnings, Balance, Celebration, Challenges, Comfort, Heart Songs, and Loss.

For those interested in the correlating Torah portions that inspired the blessings you can find this information in the Blessings for Weekly Torah Portions on page 243.

Believing in a blessing is to believe that our very presence in the world is itself the first gift, a primal blessing given freely to each of us. To be born is to be chosen. To be created and come to birth is to be blessed. We emerge into our own individuality, with a path of life opening before us through the world.

The heart of a blessing is to believe that despite all the darkness, we hope and instinctively trust that at the deepest level of reality some intimate kindness exists.

Our lives are filled with new beginnings, new difficulties and challenges. Jewish tradition teaches that all beginnings are hard. In our confusion, fear, uncertainty and pain we call upon the invisible hope of primal kindness to help us and to open pathways of possibility by renewing and activating our inner potential.

Blessings open our hearts to feelings of appreciation, consciousness, satisfaction, and humility as we recognize the many things in life we take for granted everyday.

Blessings help us affirm the positive side of life itself. They remind us of the everyday miracles that surround us and that even when things appear dark and hopeless, we are not alone. By using these blessings we experience our interconnectedness to all of life, and nurture a deeper appreciation and feelings of gratitude for the blessings that are ours each day.

Blessings are pointers, offering an orientation and a reminder that we are not alone in the universe. Blessings help us focus on the reality of finding holiness, goodness, and unexpected wonder all around us. The rituals and the code words of a blessing connect us to feelings of hope and to each other. Every blessing centers around awareness and gratitude for life itself, for the small unnoticed blessings in our lives, and sometimes for the overwhelming need to make sense out of a difficult time in our personal lives.

Dedication

To my amazing husband Bob
and my loving family –
Judy and Boaz, Mark
and Sarah, Ohr, Eitan, Lea,
Phoebe and Matilda.

You are the blessings
in my life.

I will love you
forever and ever.

A Blessing Story

Once upon a time, a long time ago, there was an Officer of the Law, a newly minted graduate of the academy, filled with pride as you can imagine, in his crisp uniform of blue with brass buttons and gold epaulets, and ribbons for swordsmanship.

If truth be told, and truth should be told in a story, he was as pompous and full of himself as he could be. Arrogant, callous even, and with his new sword gleaming at his side, bold and cold as he could be, as well.

One day he was walking his beat and heard a commotion in the alley. He ventured into the darkness and there, in the distance, he saw a man in rags. "Come forward," he commanded. "Come forward now!" But the man in rags did not come forward. "I am an Officer of the Law, and I command you to come forward!"

The man in rags still did not move. He shifted his weight from one foot to the other and spoke, "I don't know what I'm going to do with you."

"Do with me?" the Officer of the Law mocked. "Do with me? You don't do with me! I do with you! I am an Officer of the Court and I order you to come forward."

"Ahh," said the man in rags, "now I know what to do with you," and as he spoke, he drew his sword. "Now I know exactly what to do," and without another word he moved to attack.

The Officer of the Law drew his sword, of course, in defense. "Stop that!" he ordered. "Put down your sword right now or someone is going to get hurt for no reason." But the man in rags did not stop. "Stop!" he said again, but to no avail, and as the man in rags thrust his sword forward, the Officer of the Law was forced to retreat. Just as it seemed that the man in rags would actually prevail over the Officer, he suddenly lowered his guard, and what the Officer of the Law had intended as a parry became a thrust. His sword ran right through the man in rags.

"I didn't mean that," the Officer of the Law said. "I didn't mean to hurt you. Why didn't you stop when I ordered you to? Why did you attack me?"

All the man in rags could say was "I am leaving you – but as I do, I put upon you the Curse of Blessings."

"What do you mean?" asked the Officer of the Law, now quite confused by all that had happened in that narrow alleyway.

"The Curse of Blessings means that every day you must say a new blessing, one you have never said before. On the day you do not say a new blessing, on that day you will die."

The man in rags closed his eyes. The Officer of the Law looked around for help. No one was in sight. When he turned back, the man in rags had disappeared. He was gone.

"It must have been a dream or a nightmare," the Officer of the Law thought. "I imagined the whole thing."

The time was late in the afternoon. The sun was setting. As much as the Officer of the Law tried to ignore his experience he could not. It was sunset, the end of every Jewish day (after all this is a Jewish story), and the Officer of the Law suddenly felt his body growing colder and knew for certain from the chill that his life was actually leaving him.

In a panic, he uttered these words of blessing: "O my God, thank you for creating such a beautiful sunset." At once warmth and life flowed back into him. He realized, with both shock and relief, the curse had been for real.

The next morning he did not delay. He woke with words of blessing: "I bless the Source that allowed me to wake up this morning." His life felt secure the entire day. The next morning he blessed his ability to rise from his bed, the following day, that he could tie his shoes.

Day after day he found abilities he could bless: that he could go to the bathroom, that he had teeth to brush, that each finger of his hands still worked, that he had toes on his feet and hair on his head. He blessed his clothes, every garment. He blessed his house, the roof and floor, his furniture, every table and chair.

At last he ran out of things to bless, so he began to bless relationships. He blessed his family and friends, fellow workers, and those who worked for him. He blessed the mailman and the clerks, firefighters and school teachers. He was surprised to find they appreciated his blessings. His words had power. They drew family and friends closer to him. Word went out that this was an unusual Officer of the Law, one who spread blessings.

Years passed, decades. The policeman had to go farther afield to find new sources of blessing. He blessed city councils and university buildings, scientists and their discoveries. As he traveled through the world he became in awe of its balance and beauty and blessed that. He realized that the more he learned, the more he had to bless. His life was long, and he had the opportunity to learn in every field.

He passed the age of one hundred. Most of his friends were long gone. His time was relegated to searching for the purpose in his life and the one source from which all blessings flow. He had long since realized he was not the source but only the conduit, the channel, and even that realization was welcomed with a blessing that sustained him for yet another day.

As he approached the age of one hundred and twenty, he decided that his life was long enough. Even Moses had not lived longer than that. So on his birthday, he decided to utter no new blessing and allow his life to come to an end.

All that day he recited old blessings and reviewed all the blessings of his life. As the sun was setting, a chill settled into his body. He did not resist it. In the twilight, a figure appeared, the man in rags.

"You," said the Officer of the Law. "I have thought about you every day for a hundred years! I never meant to harm you. Please, forgive me."

"You still don't understand," said the man in rags. "You don't know who I am, do you? I am the angel who was sent a hundred years ago to harvest your soul, but when I looked at you, so arrogant and proud, so pompous and full of yourself, there was nothing there to harvest. An empty uniform was all I saw. So I put upon you the Curse of Blessings, and now look what you've become."

The Officer of the Law grasped in an instant all that had happened and why. Overwhelmed, he said, "Barukh ata adonai, eloheynu melekh ha'olam, shehekheyanu, vekeyemanu, vehigeyanu lazman hazeh."

"Now look what you've done!" the man in rags said in frustration. "A new blessing – the shehekheyanu."

And the policeman and the man in rags looked at each other, neither knowing what to do...

Breath Meditation

Be still and know that I am God

Be still and know that I am

Be still and know

Be still

Be

Psalm 46:11

Meditation leads us on a journey of inner awareness, a journey into our own minds, hearts, and souls. Meditation is a conscious slowing down of our very busy lives so that we can pay attention to the quieter inner world of our minds. The tools of meditation can have powerful beneficial effects in our everyday lives.

Our thoughts are powerful. A well-known meditation leader teaches, "You are what you think you are! What you find in your mind is what you put there." We all know that we cannot control the world outside, but we can pay attention to what we bring into ourselves. Insight and understanding arise from awareness, along with a sense of calm and peacefulness.

The basis for Jewish meditation is traditionally understood to come from the Torah when Elijah the Prophet experiences serious despair, feeling everything he did was a mistake. After 40 days of existential despair he arrives at Mt. Sinai and says, "God, I've messed up."

He stays alone on the mountaintop, depressed and desolate. The Torah tells us that there were four manifestations. First was the wind, the wind that smashed rocks. And the Bible said, and Elijah said, and maybe God said, "God is not in the wind." Then there was a strong earthquake from the belly of the world. And the Bible said, and Elijah said, and maybe God said, "God is not in the earthquake." And then there was a raging fire. And the Bible said, and Elijah said, and maybe God said, "God is not in the fire."

Finally there was a voice of fine silence (kol demama dakka), a voice of stillness. There was just silence. There was no voice that said, "God is not in the silence." And there was no voice that said, "God is in the silence." There was just silence.

This is the central teaching of Jewish meditation. Not in the wind (the wind is words), not in the earthquake (the earthquake is emotions and feelings), and not in the fire (the fire is religious ecstasy or imagination gone wild). We find ourselves, we become intimately aware in simple silence, in a voice of fine silence (kol demama dakka).

Each of us creates our own thoughts and our thoughts create our actions and our actions determine our characters. By becoming more conscious of our own thought processes, we become more self-reflective. We assess the way we are thinking and can choose to create a more peaceful beautiful and meaningful inner world. There are many different ways to create your own meditation practice. Simply making the decision to sit quietly for a few minutes is the first step.

Breath Meditation takes you on a journey of inner awareness by asking you to focus on your breath as your connection between your physical being and your spiritual being.

Begin by sitting quietly and notice the mechanics of a single breath. Try to breathe with your mouth closed. Feel the air around your nostrils being gently pulled into your body. Feel it warm and move down your throat as your lungs draw it in. Allow your stomach muscles to relax so that the breath fills the deep space and your belly relaxes and expands.

Experience the moment of fullness as you fill up with breath. Then feel it rise and leave your body. There is a moment of absolute stillness before your lungs pull the next breath in through your nostrils. Notice the pattern – in and full, then out and empty. Notice you can trust your lungs to keep filling you up with air, that the empty moment when all breath is expelled is a tiny death and yet, the lungs pull in the next breath and then the next and the next, bringing you back to life again and again. A tiny miracle.

After each blessing in this book, you will find a breath meditation to focus and connect you even more closely to your blessing. You can repeat the breath meditation as many times as you wish. Try to hold onto it as you go through your day. The meditation helps seal the blessing in your heart.

A BLESSING FOR LIFE'S JOURNEY

A blessing for the journey,
for the going forth and the coming back,
the first step across thresholds,
a nod to the mezuzah
guarding the gateways of our lives.

We pass through into the unknown,
step into the strange and we become strangers,
travelers, wanderers, pilgrims.
We step into the unknown journey of our lives.

We ask for strength to overcome obstacles,
confidence to make good decisions,
the ability to respond rather than react.
We ask for protection from harm,
encounters with gentle teachers
and sympathetic guides.
We ask for courage to walk through the door.

We move towards insight and clarity,
awareness, appreciation, and transformation.
We offer blessings – spoken or whispered
or thought in the stillness of our souls.

May you find blessings –
life, joy, and peace.
May you find what you seek.

Amen

Beginnings

Go forth from your place
and you shall be a blessing.

(Genesis 12:1-3)

Inner Awareness

Be aware of the moment when you know
that things must change.
Notice when the inner journey of your life
must begin,
the instant you must push back,
stand up and walk out the door.
May you begin your exploration
from wherever you are right now.
May you journey into yourself until
all your dreaming potential
becomes realized in ways yet unknown.
May you walk with hope and with courage
And make your life a blessing.

Amen

Go forth from your place
and you shall be a blessing.

(Genesis 12:1-3)

Breath Meditation for

INNER AWARENESS

This breath meditation asks you
to notice discontent in your life and awareness
that you need to make a change.

Go forth from your place
and you shall be a blessing.

(Genesis 12:1-3)

Focus and breathe in:
Go forth from your place

Focus and breathe out:
and you shall be a blessing.

Repeat Three Times

Inner Awareness

Book of Genesis 12:1-3

Torah Reading: *Lekh Lekha / Go to Yourself*

Called by the Holy One to leave home, Abraham and Sarah begin their life's journey towards insight and wholeness in Canaan. Their journey teaches them to accept the responsibility to discover and fulfill their life's purpose.

Birth

May you experience long days
of intense creativity and formation
that change you forever.
May you birth something new in this world
that never existed before.
May this creative birthing
transform you so profoundly
that you are no longer the same person.
May you step into a period of procreation so pure
that new viewpoints and insights appear to you.
From that creative moment of birthing,
of touching heaven,
may you return with a sense of accomplishment
to the ordinary world
welcomed and appreciated
for the creation you have birthed.

Amen

Such are the rituals
concerning her who bears
a child, male or female.

(Leviticus 12:7)

Breath Meditation for BIRTH

This breath meditation nurtures
your creative energy.

Such are the rituals
concerning her who bears
a child, male or female

(Leviticus 12:7)

Focus and breathe in:
Such are the rituals

Focus and breathe out:
concerning her who bears a child, male or female

Repeat Three Times

Birth

Book of Leviticus 12:1 – 13:59

Torah reading: *Tazria / Brings Forth Seed*

The various purity laws and rituals concerning childbirth establish the holiness of creating life. After giving birth, a woman remains impure until she brings offerings to the Holy One.

Rebirth

May you welcome the opportunity
to rebirth yourself
strong in your own sense of who you are,
held up by those who came before you.
May the legacy of your family ancestors
support you on your journey
as the memory of Joseph
supported Israel in the wilderness.
As your thoughts become actions in the world
and your actions create your character,
resolve to birth a better self.
May you find sure footing
on a path only you can walk
in the midst of the sea
that threatens to drown you.
May you triumph over your fears
and come through the sea onto dry land
a new soul freeing herself from the birth waters.

Amen

Israel went
on dry land
in the midst of the sea

(Exodus 14:29)

Breath Meditation for
Rebirth

This breath meditation supports you
in the inner work of change and rebirth.

Israel went on dry land
in the midst of the sea

(Exodus 14:29)

Focus and breathe in:
Israel went on dry land

Focus and breathe out:
in the midst of the sea

Repeat Three Times

REBIRTH

Book of Exodus 13:17 – 17:16

Torah reading: ***Beshallakh / Sent Away***

This is the moment of the Exodus, the Sea parts, and the people begin the process of re-creating themselves, of a communal rebirthing from slavery to freedom. Moses remembers to take Joseph's bones out of Egypt. Miriam leads the dancing, with timbrel in hand, on the other side.

Possibilities

May you open to your life's possibilities
as the baby Moses did,
floating on the primal waters of the Nile.
May you trust that your innate purpose
will reveal itself to you
during your life's journey.
May you nurture your inner self
guided by your experiences
and strengthened
by your hard won wisdom.
May you face the mystery and
learn the secrets of the wilderness,
knowing that you are held
in the loving embrace of the Holy One.

Amen

For from the water,
I drew the child out

(Exodus 2:10)

Breath Meditation for POSSIBILITIES

This breath meditation invites you to name your innermost dreams and desires.

For from the water,
I drew the child out

(Exodus 2:10)

Focus and breathe in:
For from the water

Focus and breathe out:
I drew the child out

Repeat Three Times

Possibilities

Book of Exodus 1:1 – 6:1

Torah reading: ***Shemot / Names***

The journey from slavery to freedom begins in the second book of the Torah, the book of Exodus. Moses, nurtured by extraordinary women – Yokheved (his mother), Miriam (his sister), Batya (Pharaoh's daughter), and Tzipporah (his wife) – matures into a person who understands his purpose in life, to lead the people out of Egypt.

Transformation

May you be able to hear and respond
to an inner call for transformation.
May you connect to a divine spark
in the fullness of your being.
God will be what God will be,
you will be what you will become.
Allow patience to settle inside you
as you awaken to the power of your being.
May each breath you inhale
and each beat of your heart
connect you to an inner call
for wholeness and holiness
the Oneness
at the core of your being.

Amen

I am Being
and I will take you
out from under
the burdens of Egypt

(Exodus 6:6)

Breath Meditation for TRANSFORMATION

This breath meditation helps you connect to Oneness at the core of your being.

I am Being and I will take you out
from under the burdens of Egypt

(Exodus 6:6)

Focus and breathe in:
I am Being and I will take you out

Focus and breathe out:
from under the burdens of Egypt

Repeat Three Times

Transformation

Book of Exodus 6:2 – 9:35

Torah reading: *Va-era / I Appeared*

At the burning bush, Moses begins a relationship with the Holy One. Confident in the divine promise of redemption, he leaves his desert community to confront the Pharaoh.

LEAVE

May your dreams of leaving
your family, your home, your birthplace,
connect you to the divine spark
that lives inside you.
As you pass into the unknown
and step into the strange
you become a stranger to your former self.
You walk into the unknown journey of your life
with strength to overcome obstacles
and the confidence to make good decisions.
May you find protection from harm.

May you live fully in the land of your own life
cultivating, harvesting, and sharing
the gifts that are yours.
May you never feel alone when you leave
knowing that the Holy One is with you.

Amen

I am with you wherever you go,
I will not leave you

(Genesis 28:15)

Breath Meditation to

Leave

This breath meditation reminds you that you are never completely alone.

I am with you wherever you go,
I will not leave you

(Genesis 28:15)

Focus and breathe in:
I am with you wherever you go

Focus and breathe out:
I will not leave you

Repeat Three Times

Leave

Book of Genesis 28:10 – 32:3

Torah reading: *Vayetze / And He Left*

Jacob (fearing his brother, Esau, will kill him) flees his birthplace to build a new life in Haran. There he marries Leah and Rachel and fathers twelve sons whose descendants become the twelve tribes of Israel.

Create a Family

May you follow the dream of your soul
and never give up, as Tamar never did.
May you be willing to break the rules
and stand up for yourself
and your longing to birth the future.
May you be willing to take off your veil
and stand strong and confident.
Know that the divine spark
within you will never abandon you.
May you celebrate your own strength
and cherish the power given to you
to create your own family your way.

Amen

And she rose and
went her way and took off
the veil she was wearing

(Genesis 38:19)

Breath Meditation to
Create a Family

This breath meditation invites you
to reveal yourself and follow your dreams.

And she rose and went her way
and took off the veil she was wearing

(Genesis 38:19)

Focus and breathe in:
And she rose and went her way

Focus and breathe out:
and took off the veil she was wearing

Repeat Three Times

Create a Family

Book of Genesis 37:1 – 40:23

Torah reading: *Vayeshev / And He Settled Down*

Judah, one of Joseph's brothers, tries to ensure his family's future by insisting that his surviving son marries his brother's widow, Tamar. She ensures the future of the people by marrying Judah and giving birth to twins, Zerah and Perez, ancestors of King David.

Journeys

May you be blessed on your journey,
Finding comfort and refuge as you travel.
As you step into the strange
and become a stranger,
may each traveler, wanderer, and seeker you meet
offer wisdom and empathy.
as you step into the unknown journey of your life.
May you be protected from all harm.
May you learn and grow from encounters
with gentle teachers and sympathetic guides.
May you hold onto the awareness that
you have the courage to walk away from difficult situations.
You will move towards compassion and clarity,
awareness, and appreciation.
You will find answers and more questions.
May you find what you seek.

Amen

When you cross the Jordan
you will find a place of refuge

(Numbers 35:10-11)

Breath Meditation for
JOURNEYS

This breath meditation encourages you
to learn from your journey through life.

When you cross the Jordan
you will find a place of refuge

(Numbers 35:10-11)

Focus and breathe in:
When you cross the Jordan

Focus and breathe out:
you will find a place of refuge

Repeat Three Times

Journeys

Book of Numbers 33:1 – 36:13

Torah reading: ***Massei / Journeys***

After forty years, the people have journeyed from Egypt to the east bank of the Jordan River. Now they need to find the strength to enter the promised land.

Balance

Come with me to another place
from where you can see

(Numbers 23:13)

Revelation

May you slow down long enough to notice
what your daily life reveals.
May someone close to you offer help
so that things might be better for you
as Yitro revealed to Moses.
May you let down your defenses
and take to heart
the wisdom and advice from even
the most unlikely angel.
May you be inspired
to make changes
and feel yourself lifted up
as if on eagle's wings,
protected and supported
as you integrate today's
insights and revelations.

Amen

I carried you on
the wings of eagles and
brought you to me

(Exodus 19:4)

Breath Meditation for
Revelation

This breath meditation urges you to let yourself feel held in supportive embrace as you open to small moments of revelation and insight.

I carried you on the wings of eagles
and brought you to me

(Exodus 19:4)

Focus and breathe in:
I carried you on the wings of eagles

Focus and breathe out:
and brought you to me

Repeat Three Times

Revelation

Book of Exodus 18:1 – 20:23

Torah reading: *Yitro / Jethro*

Moses struggles to become a true leader and accepts guidance and advice from Yitro, his father-in-law, the high priest of Midian. He delegates responsibility and learns to pace himself. The people remain unruly and dissatisfied even as they remember that they were lifted up out of slavery as if on the wings of an eagle.

Perseverance

May perseverance shine in you
like an eternal light in the wilderness
that keeps you going,
a beacon of encouragement
no matter how dark
the night landscape of your soul.
May you endure past the weariness
that invades your spirit
and persist
until you find refuge and safe haven.
May you tend this light,
nurturing and caring for it,
understanding that this persistent light within you
comes from an inner divine spark
that will always light your way.

Amen

Kindle a constant light,
an everlasting statute
for all time

(Exodus 27:21)

Breath Meditation for PERSEVERANCE

This breath meditation encourages you to persevere in your inner work.

Kindle a constant light,
an everlasting statute for all time

(Exodus 27:21)

Focus and breathe in:
Kindle a constant light

Focus and breathe out:
an everlasting statute for all time

Repeat Three Times

Perseverance

Book of Exodus 27:20 – 30:10

Torah reading: *Tetzaveh / Command*

The people are commanded to persevere and keep a lamp burning always in the wilderness Sanctuary. The perseverance associated with this tradition continues to the present day as the Ner Tamid, the eternal light that is found in every synagogue in the world.

Rest

May you find a sacred rhythm in your life,
a habit of punctuating your days of work
with a seventh day of absolute rest.
May the gift of rest
bless you with awareness
of what is really important to you.
May shabbat restore your soul
and offer holiness
to ease your mind
and heal your spirit.
May you play and take a walk,
enjoy food and friends
and take comfort
easy and long
in the blessing of sacred rest.

Amen

On the seventh day
there shall be holiness for you,
in a day of absolute rest

(Exodus 35:2)

Breath Meditation for REST

This breath meditation inspires you to take seriously your need for rest, an hour each day, a day each week.

On the seventh day there shall be holiness for you,
in a day of absolute rest

(Exodus 35:2)

Focus and breathe in:
On the seventh day there shall be holiness for you

Focus and breathe out:
in a day of absolute rest

Repeat Three Times

Rest

Book of Exodus 35:1 – 38:20

Torah reading: *Vayakhel / Gather*

As the portable wilderness Sanctuary takes shape under the artistic leadership of Bezalel, the people structure their work lives around a weekly day of complete and sacred rest.

Integrity

May you take an accounting
of your life day by day,
review the positive and negative
on an internal balance sheet
that ends with a commitment
to do better as you journey on.
As Moses made an accounting
to the community and to God,
may you dedicate yourself,
hold yourself accountable
to the work you have been called to do.
May your daily accounting
find the good you do
outweighs your mistakes
and is of great value in this world.

Amen

Everyone counted,
from the age of maturity
and upwards.

(Exodus 38:26)

Breath Meditation for INTEGRITY

This breath meditation reminds you to be a person of integrity every day.

Everyone counted,
from the age of maturity and upwards

(Exodus 38:26)

Focus and breathe in:
Everyone counted,

Focus and breathe out:
from the age of maturity and upwards

Repeat Three Times

Integrity

Book of Exodus 38:21 – 40:38

Torah reading: *Pekuday / Accounting*

Moses is in charge of keeping the records and accounts as the people continue to craft the Sanctuary. According to tradition, he demanded that others hold him to the highest accounting standards, so that no one could doubt his integrity.

Balance

May you hear the call to live a life of balance
between the demands of daily worldly life
and the inner work of your soul.
May you not get too distracted
or distant from the source of everything.
May you bring forward offerings
the first fruits of your life
from a place of balance.
May you adopt organizing principles for your life,
mitzvot that bring you closer to wholeness.
May you shine in harmony
with the divine spark
that glows within you.

Amen

You shall bring forward
an offering of your first fruits

(Leviticus 2:14)

Breath Meditation for BALANCE

This breath meditation asks you to create a balanced life in tune with nature.

You shall bring forward
an offering of your first fruits

(Leviticus 2:14)

Focus and breathe in:
You shall bring forward

Focus and breathe out:
an offering of your first fruits

Repeat Three Times

Balance

Book of Leviticus 1:1 – 5:26

Torah reading: *Vayikra / And He Called*

Leviticus centers and balances the Torah (two books precede it and two books follow it). Vayikra offers a manual for holiness in our personal and communal lives.

Cleansing

May you find a private time in your daily life
that you can hold onto
for reflection and meditation.
A regular time of quiet seclusion
allows and encourages inner growth.
Pay close attention
to your need for inner change
that may manifest as outer confusion
and indecision.
Step out of ordinary time
and discover it is possible
to reimagine some aspect of your life.
Don't be distracted by the demands of others,
recognize your irritability as an inner need
to shift and set something deep within you free.
Then, immerse in a ritual bath
or simply wash your hands
as you return to the demands of your life
cleansed and ready to experience
expansion and renewal.

Amen

Then bathe in fresh water,
and you shall be clean

(Leviticus 15:13)

Breath Meditation for CLEANSING

This breath meditation offers water purification rituals to cleanse and refresh your body, mind and spirit.

Then bathe in fresh water,
and you shall be clean

(Leviticus 15:13)

Focus and breathe in:
Then bathe in fresh water,

Focus and breathe out:
and you shall be clean

Repeat Three Times

Cleansing

Book of Leviticus 14:1 – 15:33

Torah reading: *Metzora / Disease*

Individuals separate from the community to perform purification rituals and are then welcomed back into the community.

Imperfection

May you acknowledge your imperfections
in your own words
and reveal to yourself
who you really are.
Offer up the defects,
small failures and habits
that restrict and confine your spirit.
May you find self-acceptance
in the very limitations of being human,
in your flaws, cracks, and wrinkles.
Dream of perfect repair and wholeness
and envision yourself as a holy spirit.
May you reach a place of honest acceptance
between what might be
and what is.
This is the way the world cleanses itself.

Amen

Having a defect,
you still may eat of holy food

(Leviticus 21:21-22)

Breath Meditation for IMPERFECTION

This breath meditation invites you to accept your imperfections and feel worthy as you bless and eat holy food.

Having a defect,
you still may eat of holy food

(Leviticus 21:21-22)

Focus and breathe in:
Having a defect

Focus and breathe out:
you still may eat of holy food

Repeat Three Times

Imperfection

Book of Leviticus 21:1 – 24:23

Torah reading: ***Emor / Say***

Ritual behavior including offering and eating holy food helps us face our imperfections and instill holiness in ourselves.

Simplify

May you stand unencumbered on the mountain
feeling the wind blow the hair
back from your face.
When you return from that height
may you understand
that possessions and obligations
weigh you down
and trap you in never enough.
Trust that you can live well with less.
Heed the call on that mountain to simplify
and return to the Holy One.
Know every living thing needs freedom to rest
and so do you.

Amen

You shall live upon it
in security

(Leviticus 25:18)

Breath Meditation to SIMPLIFY

This breath meditation encourages you to simplify your life.

You shall live upon it

in security

(Leviticus 25:18)

Focus and breathe in:
You shall live upon it

Focus and breathe out:
in security

Repeat Three Times

SIMPLIFY

Book of Leviticus 25:1 – 26:2

Torah reading: ***Behar/ On the Mountain***

The people are told to simplify their lives and give their fields and vineyards "a complete rest" every seventh year, eating only what grows from the uncultivated ground.

PROMISES

May you make promises with care
knowing that your words are sacred.
May you be known as one
who honors what you say and inspires trust.
May the words of your mouth
reflect the meditations of your heart.
Allow reflection when anger heats your soul.
Encourage time to pass between
striking a match
and lighting a flame.
Acknowledge your own responsibility
for vows and pledges.
May you recognize the power of what you say
and stand by your verbal commitments.

Amen

If you make a vow,
you shall not break
your word

(Numbers 30:3)

Breath Meditation for
PROMISES

This breath meditation invites you
to inspire others to trust you.

If you make a vow,
you shall not break your word

(Numbers 30:3)

Focus and breathe in:
If you make a vow

Focus and breathe out:
you shall not break your word

Repeat Three Times

Promises

Book of Numbers 30:2 – 32:42

Torah reading: *Mattot / Tribes*

We learn the biblical rules governing promises (vows and oaths). The power of words to hurt and to heal cannot be underestimated.

Empowerment

Stand strong in your commitment
to shape your own reality,
to discern the boundaries between
the hidden and the revealed.
Keep your heart open
and your relationship with divine Mystery
will deepen and mature.
Keep your heart strong
and you will shape and create
reality from what is good and true.
Be steadfast and whole in your heart
and you will be empowered to
reject loss and emptiness
and choose life and its fullness.
The choice is yours.

Amen

God will take you back
in love

(Deuteronomy 30:3)

Breath Meditation for EMPOWERMENT

This breath meditation encourages you to trust the choices you make.

God will take you back
in love

(Deuteronomy 30:3)

Focus and breathe in:
God will take you back

Focus and breathe out:
in love

Repeat Three Times

Empowerment

Book of Deuteronomy 29:9 – 30:20

Torah reading: *Nitzavim / Standing*

Moses completes his final talk to the people, urging them to make good choices in their lives. He assures them that even when they make mistakes, God will always forgive and love them.

Listening

Listen to the song of the breath.
God breathes in with a cosmic sigh,
and when the Holy One breathes out,
you instinctively expand and breathe in.
One shared sigh, one rhythm of release.

Breathe in the shema
soft inhale of holy breath,
allow holiness to enter your heart.

Breathe out ekhad
one into One – union and unity
held together in a kiss of breath.

Hear the call to listen and know
we are all connected,
bound in intimate union of breath.
Effortlessly linked in one shared sigh,
one rhythm of release.

Amen

Listen and hear
your life's song

(Deuteronomy 32:44)

Breath Meditation for LISTENING

This breath meditation invites you to listen to the essential underlying oneness of life.

Listen and hear

your life's song

(Deuteronomy 32:44)

Focus and breathe in:
Listen and hear

Focus and breathe out:
your life's song

Repeat Three Times

LISTENING

Book of Deuteronomy 32:1 – 32:52

Torah reading: ***Ha'azinu / Listen***

Moses recites God's prophetic poem to all the people. The poem is the song of his life and his last contact with the people he led from slavery to freedom. He then ascends Mount Nebo to view the promised land before he dies.

Celebrations

This is the day
the Holy One has made,
let us rejoice and be glad in it

(Psalm 118:24)

Your Birthday

Blessed be the source
that dreamed the day
of your presence here on earth.
May you feel embraced,
enfolded anew
by the miracle of your being.
May you find the deep purpose of your soul
loved and cherished into becoming
who you are meant to be.
May inevitable dark gifts
of hurt and loss
school you in
strength and perseverance.
May you find holiness
when you look into the eyes
of someone who loves you.
May you be a source of holiness for others.
May you treasure and develop your uniqueness
and be a blessing to all you meet.

Amen

Anniversary

May you be blessed as you celebrate today,
filled with gratitude for all the joy
that you have experienced in your lives,
from the day you celebrated
the union of your hearts
up to the present day.

May you always be grateful
that you have one another
and that you are able to express your love
in acts of kindness.
May you continue to heal the hurts
and forgive their cause.
May you waste no opportunity
to speak words
of sympathy and appreciation
praise and love
to each other and to those
who are precious to you.
As you celebrate today
may you enjoy a length of days,
a ripe and full old age together.

Amen

Yom Kippur

May you be able to forgive yourself
and from that place of compassion
offer the same to others.

May you remember that "I'm sorry"
is a prayer and listen in wonder
to the sound of your heart crying.

May you follow a path
that leads to forgiveness,
where you walk to the rhythm
of your own strength and courage.

May you feel the whole world
open inside you as you accept and forgive
yourself for being exactly who you are.

May you surround yourself
with life-affirming companions and dear souls
who sustain all the good that is within you.

May the gates of forgiveness
always swing open for you
as you open into humility and compassion.

May the year ahead be sweet
and filled with purpose
as you welcome God's presence
on your journey.

Amen

HANUKKAH

As you kindle your own lights,
call forth a revelation
of the hidden and intense light
that shone in Eden
when Adam and Eve were bathed
in the Primordial light of creation.

As you kindle the lights of Hanukkah
you become a guardian of light,
a guardian of the world at Hanukkah.
May you sustain, nurture and guard this light.
May your further acts be
of creation and illumination.
May you recognize that you hold
a spark of hidden light
deep within you
with the power to transform,
illumine and heal.

You are a beacon of hope
dispelling darkness with wisdom.
May you encourage your light
to shine with radiance,
triumph over negativity
and push back darkness.

Amen

Passover

May you remember the miraculous
in your own life this Passover.
May you understand that you can pass
through narrow and difficult places inside you,
that Egypt in Hebrew means
through a tight and dangerous place.

When you eat matzah
the bread of affliction
may you take a bite out of
that which afflicts you.
May you chew away at it
layer by layer
until you clear a channel
for your soul to feel open and free.

May you always walk
purposefully through life
as we did at the parting of the sea,
for movement without direction
will create just a hole in the ground.
May you remember freedom is
a state of mind, not a place.
May all your matzah balls be light.
May you celebrate until you are all joy.

Amen

Thanksgiving

For the gift of your own life breath,
for the joy of this company,
for the delight of the food on this table,
for those who prepared this meal
Thank you Source of All.

For friends old and new
and family near and far
and the chance each new day
to make a difference
Thank you

For the redemptive power in nature
the goodness of the earth
the insight to walk upon her lightly
and repair and restore her bounty
Thank you

For the gift of each new day
that brings the hope of healing
for spirit, soul and body
to transcend suffering
Thank you

For the roof overhead and
the clothes on your back
for laughter and celebration
and the voices of the children
Thank you

For all your many blessings
for the freedom you enjoy
to gather in any faith and language and
for the help that you can offer
to those in need
Thank you

Amen

CHALLENGES

And you wrestled with yourself
until the break of dawn

(Genesis 32:25)

Family Relationships

May you open your family's wells
and dive deep beneath the surface
to explore the struggles
waiting in your past.
Know that your present actions determine
your past and your past becomes your future.
May you rise to the surface
understanding that our lives
are bound up with each other
and that the same well waters us all.
May your thirst be satisfied
as you drink deeply
of shared stories and struggles.
May you clear away obstructions
and connect to the source
of flowing blessings.

Amen

And they found there
a well of living water

(Genesis 26:19)

Breath Meditation for
FAMILY RELATIONSHIPS

This breath meditation encourages you
to deepen your family relationships
and dive beneath the surface.

And they found there
a well of living water

(Genesis 26:19)

Focus and breathe in:
And they found there

Focus and breathe out:
a well of living water

Repeat Three Times

Family Relationships

Book of Genesis 25:19 – 28:9

Torah reading: *Toldot / Generations*

Isaac, a quiet man who never leaves the land of Israel, gets little attention in the Torah. He opens up his father's wells, a metaphor for opening to wisdom, and passes on blessings to his son, Jacob.

STRUGGLE

May you struggle with your false self
and confront the mystery
at the core of your being.
May you be held in the grip of truth
until all your self-deceptions melt away,
your delusions fade
and your defenses fall.
May the dawn break as it did for Jacob
revealing the hidden radiance
that shines through
all the veils and masks
so that you know who you really are.
May your soul call to you
and send you a new name.

Amen

And you wrestled with yourself
until the break of dawn.

(Genesis 32:25)

Breath Meditation for STRUGGLE

This breath meditation supports
your struggles with your inner demons.

And you wrestled with yourself
until the break of dawn

(Genesis 32:25)

Focus and breathe in:
And you wrestled with yourself

Focus and breathe out:
until the break of dawn

Repeat Three Times

Struggle

Book of Genesis 32:4 – 36:43

Torah reading: ***Vayishlakh / and He was Sent***

After twenty years in exile, Jacob returns home. On his journey Jacob pauses at the river Jabbok. He struggles with a divine being all night and earns a new name for himself, "one who struggles with God" - Israel.

Family Tension

May you find the courage to face
the struggles in your past
so that you can make peace
with those close to you
as Joseph made peace with his brothers.
May you feel strong enough to allow
acceptance to transcend bitterness.
May you begin the work of healing
by refusing to carry old hurts any longer.
May a well of forgiveness for yourself and for others
allow healing tears to flow down your cheeks.
May you be blessed with a heart of compassion.

Amen

Let us rise and go,
that we may live and not die

(Genesis 43:8)

Breath Meditation for
Family Tension

This breath meditation, invites you
to make peace with those close to you.

Let us rise and go,
that we may live and not die

(Genesis 43:8)

Focus and breathe in:
Let us rise and go,

Focus and breathe out:
that we may live and not die

Repeat Three Times

Family Tension

Book of Genesis 41:1 – 44:17

Torah reading: ***Miketz / At the End***

Family tensions and tangles weave through the Joseph story: jealousy, responsibility, greed, estrangement. In this story of seething family emotions, intimations of evil and destruction are exchanged for good.

RECONCILE

May your life's journey be woven with dreams
and may you discern your mission to make
life better as Joseph did.
May you live in full acceptance of who you are.
May any harm you have done intentionally or not
be put to rest by forgiving yourself
and those who love you.
May you be able to take off your mask,
feel humility and awareness that
the love that we hold in our hearts
is not our possession
and it is not for us to reward or withhold.
Weep aloud,
cleanse and forgive yourself.
May you recognize your life's experiences
as the source of your own heart of compassion.

Amen

God has sent me before you
to preserve life

(Genesis 45:5)

Breath Meditation to RECONCILE

This breath meditation asks you to forgive yourself for any harm you caused another and reconcile with those you hold in your heart.

God has sent me before you
to preserve life

(Genesis 45:5)

Focus and breathe in:
God has sent me before you

Focus and breathe out:
to preserve life

Repeat Three Times

Reconcile

Book of Genesis 44:18 – 47:27

Torah reading: *Vayigash / Come Near*

Joseph reconciles with his brothers and with his father, Jacob, inviting them to live under his protection and care in Egypt. The family leaves a desperate famine in Israel for food and safety in Egypt, secure in the promise that God will someday lead them out of Egypt back to the holy land.

Freedom

May you come into the recesses
and deep places
of your heart
to soften and free yourself
from oppression.
May you find the courage
to face your inner Pharaoh
(the heaviness you carry around),
and know you will find your way to freedom.
May you soften and float out from under
the burdens that weigh you down.
May the narrow straits of Egypt (Mitzrayim)
become the birth canal of your new free self.
Awaken to your own power
to turn fear into love
aware that the Holy One
sustains and supports you.

Amen

Remember this day,
when you went out of Egypt

(Exodus 13:3)

Breath Meditation for FREEDOM

This breath meditation helps you focus on the inner burdens that oppress you.

Remember this day,
when you went out of Egypt

(Exodus 13:3)

Focus and breathe in:
Remember this day

Focus and breathe out:
when you went out of Egypt

Repeat Three Times

Freedom

Book of Exodus 10:1 – 13:16

Torah reading: *Bo / Come*

Moses faces Pharaoh again and again to demand the people's release. At tremendous cost (the plague of the death of the firstborn), the people are allowed to leave. Moses emerges as a strong leader, aware of the high price of freedom.

Stand Up

May you be known as one who is willing
to stand up and be counted.
Do what you can to contribute
to the well-being of others,
and find comfort in knowing that others
are making contributions as well.
May you never worship false values
or build a golden calf in moments
when you feel worthless and abandoned.
May you never delude yourself,
but remain aware
of your own value and potential,
your own inner divine spark,
that keeps you centered and secure
in your beliefs and values.

Amen

I know you by name,
you have found favor
in my eyes

(Exodus 33:12)

Breath Meditation to

STAND UP

This breath meditation encourages you
to stand up for what is right and be counted.

I know you by name,
you have found favor in my eyes

(Exodus 33:12)

Focus and breathe in:
I know you by name

Focus and breathe out:
you have found favor in my eyes

Repeat Three Times

Stand Up

Book of Exodus 30:11 – 34:35

Torah reading: *Ki Tissa / When You Count*

After each person contributes to the building of the Sanctuary, Moses ascends Mount Sinai to receive the two tablets inscribed with the Ten Commandments. He is gone for so long that the people build a surrogate golden calf, because they feel abandoned.

Resistance

When you journey through
the innermost terrain of your being,
dare to confront your shadow self
as relentless winds of self-disclosure
reveal your truth and scour you clean.
May you overcome mountains of resistance
and deserts of ambivalence
that try to wear you down.
Honor your hard won victories
and mourn your losses.
Know that you are safe
in the core of your being
surrounded by holy guardians
pledged to protect you
as the tribes in the desert protected the Ark.
Allow your defenses to fall
and abandon your disguises.
Commit yourself to your soul's wilderness journey
to understand and fulfill your purpose in the world.

Amen

Who you are is known in the wilderness

(Numbers 1:19)

Breath Meditation for
Resistance

This breath meditation encourages you to find yourself in your inner wilderness.

Who you are is known
in the wilderness

(Numbers 1:19)

Focus and breathe in:
Who you are is known

Focus and breathe out:
in the wilderness

Repeat Three Times

Resistance

Book of Numbers 1:2 – 4:20

Torah reading: Bamidbar / In the Wilderness

The people will mature and grow wise and old as they escort the Ark of the Covenant through the desert wilderness.

Heavy Burdens

Know that others bear the same burdens you do
and find comfort
in the shared experience of being human.
May you see that your longings and desires
are only hindrances on your journey towards light.
You are not alone in facing hungers and yearnings
that threaten to overtake you.
May you face your own shortcomings and
raise them up to the light.
May you see your heavy burdens as obstacles
you can overcome and deal with.
May you recognize your own fears,
your cravings and your restlessness,
and through awareness and acceptance,
diminish their power over your inner peace.
May you feel the light of the Holy One
Raise you up and lighten your burdens.

Amen

Others share the burden with you; you shall not bear it alone

(Numbers 11:17)

Breath Meditation for
Heavy Burdens

This breath meditation offers comfort
for the burdens you bear.

Others share the burden with you;
you shall not bear it alone

(Numbers 11:17)

Focus and breathe in:
Others share the burden with you

Focus and breathe out:
you shall not bear it alone

Repeat Three Times

Heavy Burdens

Book of Numbers 8:1 – 12:16

Torah reading: Beha'alotekha / Raise Up

We continue the difficult wilderness journey with the people. They complain and cry for a return to better days.

Doubt

May you be blessed to glimpse a vision
of your own personal honey sweet promised land.
May you cherish and hold onto
the clarity of your dream
and believe in its promise
even as it slips into memory.
May you resist the doubts that settle in,
trying to deny and undermine your dream.
May you overcome your own
resistance and ambivalence that
fill you with the terror of failing.
Know that you can defeat your doubts and fears
because you are surrounded and protected
by the Holy One as you journey towards
your honey soaked dream.

Amen

We have seen the land;
it does flow with
milk and honey

(Numbers 13:27)

Breath Meditation for

Doubt

This breath meditation helps you diminish feelings of doubt.

We have seen the land;
it does flow with milk and honey

(Numbers 13:27)

Focus and breathe in:
We have seen the land;

Focus and breathe out:
it does flow with milk and honey

Repeat Three Times

Doubt

Book of Numbers 13:1 – 15:41

Torah reading: ***Shelakh Lekha / Send for Yourself***

Forty days after Moses appoints scouts to see if the land of Canaan really is "flowing with milk and honey" the scouts return filled with doubts. All the people begin to lose faith and doubt that they can succeed in settling the land.

Challenges

Accept the times when the challenger
hidden deep inside you
bursts forth with rebellious questions.
Search out the fires that motivate
an uprising in your soul.
Recognize the passion and energy that
accompany you on life's journey.
Harness its power even as it
exposes your deepest fears and doubts.
Do not fear its arrogant power
or consuming need to take over and destroy.
It is holy work to channel this power.
You need feel no guilt because of it.
Face the fires of confrontation
with strength and conviction
and emerge powerful and clear.

Amen

The holy will be known
and the holy will be gathered

(Numbers 16:5)

Breath Meditation for CHALLENGES

This breath meditation strengthens
your resolve to address challenges in your life.

The holy will be known
and the holy will be gathered

(Numbers 16:5)

Focus and breathe in:
The holy will be known

Focus and breathe out:
the holy will be gathered close

Repeat Three Times

Challenges

Book of Numbers 16:1 – 18:32

Torah reading: ***Korakh / Korakh***

Part of the wilderness journey leads to rebellion and mutiny. Korakh (Moses' cousin) challenges Moses' exclusive authority.

Justice

Give voice to your heart's demands
for justice and truth.
Be aware of your own rights,
let no one diminish you
least of all yourself.
Do not deny your own value,
speak up for yourself
as the daughters did.
Shake off the plague of powerlessness
and rise above ambivalent feelings
to ride the rising tide of your own convictions.
The Holy One moves through you and guides you
towards justice and right action.
Know that your sense of what is fair and just
is God calling you to stand up
for yourself and for others.
You are not alone
your voice will be heard.

Amen

The plea of the daughters is just

(Numbers 27:6)

Breath Meditation for

Justice

This breath meditation reminds you
to stand up for yourself and seek justice.

The plea of the daughters
is just

(Numbers 27:6)

Focus and breathe in:
The plea of the daughters

Focus and breathe out:
is just

Repeat Three Times

Justice

Book of Numbers 25:10 – 30:1

Torah reading: Pinkhas / Pinkhas

Another census is ordered, so that all tribal lands can be allocated after the conquest. Five daughters bring their claim to inherit their family land to Moses and God upholds their claim as just.

Release

Don't hold onto the past, go out and close the door.
Allow yourself to separate
from relationships that pull you down
and the demands of others
who claimed you in the past.
Let go of hoarding and of greed,
of acquisitions and of lusting.
Recognize your inner battles with desires,
habits, addictions, and longings.
Have the strength to sever the chains
of roles that keep you captive and enslaved.
Cultivate wholeness and honesty
As you go on to create your own future.

Amen

If you no longer want her,
release her completely

(Deuteronomy 21:14)

Breath Meditation for RELEASE

This breath meditation reminds you
to let go – to release yourself and others
from roles that do not serve you well.

If you no longer want her,
release her completely

(Deuteronomy 21:14)

Focus and breathe in:
If you no longer want her,

Focus and breathe out:
release her completely

Repeat Three Times

Release

Book of Deuteronomy 21:10 – 25:19

Torah reading: *Ki Taytze/ When you go out*

A long list of laws teaches us how to create and maintain a just society. Laws include: releasing captive women, loans, divorce, treatment of vulnerable members of society, honest weights and measures and honest interest rates – to name just a few.

Comfort

It will go well with you
and your children after you

(Deuteronomy 4:40)

Healing from Chronic Illness

May you find courage and strength
to face your illness,
and hope for healing that will embrace you in life.
As you struggle with chronic illness
your health impaired and
your life in jeopardy
May you receive the blessing
that Miriam received when her brother Moses asked
El na refanah lah – God, please heal her.

May a healing Presence remain with human healers
shining a light on their efforts to succeed
in their struggle to treat disease
and find safe treatments.
Keep them on the path of health and life.

May those who care for the chronically ill
and attend to their needs
find perseverance, patience and compassion
as they labor to ease the lives of those
who look to them for comfort and well-being.

May you find compassion and understanding
acceptance and hope
for yourself and others
as worthy recipients
of concern and love.

May the day come soon when chronic disease
shall not afflict our children
and all of us are liberated
from the shadow of its terror.

Amen

Trust

May you rest in comfort and safety
when all around you seems
edging towards collapse.
May you trust that the Holy One holds you
cradled in the curve of the rainbow.
May you move ahead into the unknown
even when everyone around you seems to be drowning.
May you relax into whatever is,
releasing doubt, replacing fear with trust.
May the blessing of a great technicolor promise
Invite you to surrender in deep safety
knowing you are held in a divine embrace.

Amen

When the rainbow
is in the clouds,
I will see it

(Genesis 9:16)

Breath Meditation for TRUST

This breath meditation invites you
to trust promises, to feel safely held
in the curve of a rainbow.

When the rainbow is in the clouds,
I will see it

(Genesis 9:16)

Focus and breathe in:
When the rainbow is in the clouds

Focus and breathe out:
I will see it

Repeat Three Times

Trust

Book of Genesis 6:9 – 11:32

Torah reading: ***Noah / Rest***

When humanity fails to live up to its potential, a flood sweeps away all living beings. Finally, the deluge subsides and Noah's ark rests safely. The rainbow appears as the symbol of the Holy One's eternal promise to sustain humanity forever.

Angels

May you be aware of the presence
of angels in your life
every moment, every day.
May you remain receptive and open
to possibilities and potentiality in your life.
May you open your heart
and watch with eagerness
for opportunities to help and care for others,
to be an angel in someone's life
as an expression of your generosity.
May you sense the presence of angels
in a stranger's smile,
in a moment of unexpected support.

Amen

When he saw them,
he ran to meet them

(Genesis 18:2)

Breath Meditation for
Angels

This breath meditation reminds you
to trust the presence of angels in your life.

When he saw them,
he ran to meet them

(Genesis 18:2)

Focus and breathe in:
When he saw them

Focus and breathe out:
he ran to meet them

Repeat Three Times

Angels

Book of Genesis 18:1 – 22:24

Torah reading: *Vayera / And He Saw*

Abraham notices strangers approaching and rushes to offer them hospitality. The strangers are angels come to inform Abraham and Sarah that they will have a child, Isaac, despite their old age and loss of hope.

Loneliness

May you offer your heart freely to others
in kindness and compassion.
May loneliness lessen as you connect
to the sacred place inside you
where holiness dwells always.
When you struggle to stay connected
reject the illusion of separateness
so prevalent in the world,
know that you are not alone.
Holiness lives within you,
available and accessible
in the inner chambers of your heart.
May you make a dwelling place for Presence
And take comfort.

Amen

*Make a dwelling place for me,
that I may live with you*

(Exodus 25:8)

Breath Meditation for

Loneliness

This breath meditation assures you that you are never alone.

Make a dwelling place for me,
that I may live with you

(Exodus 25:8)

Focus and breathe in:
Make a dwelling place for me

Focus and breathe out:
that I may live with you

Repeat Three Times

Loneliness

Book of Exodus 25:1 – 27:19

Torah reading: *Terumah / Offering*

The people build a Sanctuary, a sacred space, where they can feel reassured that the Holy One is present among them. Everyone makes an offering from their heart, and senses holy Presence as they journey on.

Warmth

May you tend to the fire burning
in the recesses of your soul.
Like a priest tending an altar
may you tend to your heart,
feeding it and stirring it
until your life itself
supports and spreads sacred warmth
to cold and lonely places inside you,
to neglected relationships and old ghosts.
May the love that you give
and the love that you receive
fuel your heart so that
your fire burns pure and strong.

Amen

A constant fire
shall keep burning
on the altar.

(Leviticus 6:6)

Breath Meditation for
Warmth

This breath meditation warms the heart
until it opens in compassion.

A constant fire
shall keep burning on the altar

(Leviticus 6:6)

Focus and breathe in:
A constant fire

Focus and breathe out:
shall keep burning on the altar

Repeat Three Times

Warmth

Book of Leviticus 6:1 – 8:36

Torah reading: *Tzav / Command*

The people learn the purifying power of
bringing an offering to the Sanctuary fire.

PROTECTION

May you be protected from false accusations
and the mean-spiritedness of others.
May you walk through life shielded
against jealousy and bitterness.
Know that you are safe
from humiliation and suspicion,
because you answer only
to the divine within you.
May the Holy One help you find strength
to face and acknowledge pain and hurt
and then move past it.
May you come to understand what hides
beneath the angry passions of others,
secure in your own inner wholeness and integrity.
May you overcome needy feelings
that threaten your inner peace.
Allow the Holy One to lift you up
and help you to respond
with acceptance and compassion.

Amen

Be immune to harm
from this water of bitterness

(Numbers 5:19)

Breath Meditation for PROTECTION

This breath meditation offers protection from the harmful words and actions of others.

Be immune to harm

from this water of bitterness

(Numbers 5:19)

Focus and breathe in:
Be immune to harm

Focus and breathe out:
from this water of bitterness

Repeat Three Times

Protection

Book of Numbers 4:21 – 7:89

Torah reading: *Naso / Lift Up*

A woman accused of adultery by her jealous husband is subjected to a ritual which reminds us of our need for protection from the anger and suspicion of others.

Mistakes

When you make a mistake
familiar and often repeated
try and understand its cause.
When you disappoint yourself
hold yourself with compassion.
Offer your hard-won insights
on the fires of truth
to cleanse and purify your soul.
May you gain awareness
of the losses you fear
that keep you feeling like an outsider.
Know that mistakes and errors of judgment
can be transformed,
as the Israelites did in the wilderness
so that you can do the difficult work of acceptance.
Ask yourself what will release your guilt and shame,
what will fill the emptiness inside you?
Use the words "I'm sorry" and "I made a mistake"
as your invitation to humility and your opportunity
to grow from your experience.

Amen

You who are impure
shall purify yourself
and be pure

(Numbers 19:12)

Breath Meditation for MISTAKES

This breath meditation promises that
you can move on after you make a mistake.

You who are impure shall purify yourself
and be pure

(Numbers 9:12)

Focus and breathe in:
You who are impure shall purify yourself

Focus and breathe out:
and be pure.

Repeat Three Times

Mistakes

Book of Numbers 19:1 – 22:1

Torah reading: ***Khukat / Rules***

The mysterious ritual of the Red Heifer purifies someone who made mistakes and feels contaminated.

Feeling Loved

Hold onto your belief in love
and know that you are loved by an endless love
that flows through you to your children
and to all beings and forms of life.
Trust in the loving Presence
that waits for your heart to open.
You have so much, release old demands
and preconceived ideas of what you need.
Don't allow expectations to blind you
to the gifts in your life right now.
You don't need to roll a rock uphill
or cross the Jordan.
Know that you have love in your life
and come home to your heart.

Amen

It will go well with you
and your children after you

(Deuteronomy 4:40)

Breath Meditation to FEELING LOVED

This breath meditation promises that love transcends everything.

It will go well with you
and your children after you

(Deuteronomy 4:40)

Focus and breathe in:
It will go well with you

Focus and breathe out:
and your children after you

Repeat Three Times

Feeling Loved

Book of Deuteronomy 3:23 – 7:11

Torah reading: *Va'etkhannan / I Pleaded*

This week, Moses offers his second discourse, continuing to review the past forty years. Moses reminds the people of their sacred covenant and we read the Shema, the central declaration of Jewish faith in the Holy One, and the Ve-Ahavta, the charge to feel loved and to love God with an open heart.

Contentment

Notice the small perfect moments in your day,
the dolphin arching in playful water games,
the satisfying trill of a bird's song.
Notice when serenity surrounds you,
enfolds you in soft warm security.
Enter into the peace of these moments humbly.
Know you have found the promised land
at least for a while.
Let these unexpected moments of blessing
keep you safe from the storm.
Rest in the peace of nature
and accept the love that is
your birthright and your inheritance.

Amen

All blessings
shall come upon you
and take effect

(Deuteronomy 28:2)

Breath Meditation for CONTENTMENT

This breath meditation
inspires contentment.

All blessings shall come upon you
and take effect

(Deuteronomy 28:2)

Focus and breathe in:
All blessings shall come upon you

Focus and breathe out:
and take effect

Repeat Three Times

Contentment

Book of Deuteronomy 26:1 – 29:8

Torah portion of *Ki Tavo / When You Enter*

This week we continue the review of the laws that Moses describes as the basis of a just society when the people cross over the Jordan. He describes a ritual of welcome as they enter, dividing the twelve tribes into two choruses, facing each other.

Heart Songs

*When you have eaten your fill,
give thanks*

(Deuteronomy 8:10)

Wholeness

You are meant to be whole
to be true to your best self.
You are meant to be holy
no matter what path your life has taken.
Today, right now,
you are called to the good
to walk the path of holiness.
You are given this gift as your birthright
as one created in the image
of the Holy One.
Notice the presence of holiness
at the core of each moment.
Open your heart to the possibility
of unasked for love
celebrating your essential being,
kind and generous,
giving and compassionate.

Amen

You shall be holy,
for I am holy

(Leviticus 19:2)

Breath Meditation for WHOLENESS

This breath meditation reminds you to walk the path of holiness.

You shall be holy,
for I am holy

(Leviticus 19:2)

Focus and breathe in:
You shall be holy

Focus and breathe out:
for I am holy

Repeat Three Times

Wholeness

Book of Leviticus 19:1 – 20:27

Torah reading: *Kedoshim / Holy Ones*

The Torah teaches each of us to walk the path of wholeness and holiness to do the right thing in four categories: protect the weak, ensure social stability and justice, preserve ritual observance, and respect nature and the natural order.

Intuition

Honor the truth hidden deep inside you
made known to you through intuition.
Trust the wisdom of your body mind
as a way to sense divine Presence beyond intellect.
Let the quickened beating of your heart inform you;
the sharp intake of breath teach you;
the clarity of your eyes reveal visions.
Trust that you really can see angels
as you move from place to place.
Moments of divine truth will break through,
not from your mind alone,
but from your heart.
Allow prophecy to flow through you
in a deep connection of sinews and bones,
nerves and gut feelings.
God speaks to you through your intuition.

Amen

Come with me
to another place
from where you can see.

(Numbers 23:13)

Breath Meditation for INTUITION

This breath meditation inspires you to trust your sense of intuition.

Come with me to another place
from where you can see

(Numbers 23:13)

Focus and breathe in:
Come with me to another place

Focus and breathe out:
from where you can see

Repeat Three Times

Intuition

Book of Numbers 22:2 – 25:9

Torah reading: ***Balak / Balak***

The prophet Balaam is blind to an angel's presence even his own donkey can see. Finally, Balaam trusts his intuition. He sees the angel, and his whole worldview changes.

Clarity

May the doubts of darkness
give way to the consciousness of light.
May you be blessed with clarity,
wrapped and protected
in garments of light
May the glow of awareness
illumine your life
as light pierces the darkness,
separating day from night.
May you become a source
of wise consciousness
touching others
through your ability to see clearly
lit by an inner knowing.

Amen

And God saw the light,
that it was good

(Genesis 1:4)

Breath Meditation for
Clarity

This breath meditation invites you to feel
filled with light, with a divine spark, an inner radiance.

And God saw the light,
that it was good

(Genesis 1:4)

Focus and breathe in:
And God saw the light

Focus and breathe out:
that it was good

Repeat Three Times

Clarity

Book of Genesis 1:1 – 6:8

Torah reading: ***Bereshit / In the Beginning***

In the Beginning the Holy One speaks the world into existence. After Adam and Eve untangle into differentiated beings, they awaken to desire. The Holy One dresses them in garments of light as they leave Eden and the human drama begins.

Exuberance

May you celebrate the excesses of youth,
and revel without constraint or concern
about the limitations of being human.
May you move with great confidence towards
the spirit of possibility and what you might do.
May you cherish exuberance and ecstasy
and naïve belief in causes yet unproven,
as Nadav and Avihu did
when they rushed with their fire-pans
to offer strange fire to God.
May you commit yourself without reservation
to the passions of your life.

Amen

Each took his fire-pan
and brought forth strange fire

(Leviticus 10:1)

Breath Meditation for EXUBERANCE

This breath meditation encourages exuberant energy and passion.

Each took his fire-pan
and brought forth strange fire

(Leviticus 10:1)

Focus and breathe in:
Each took his fire-pan

Focus and breathe out:
and brought forth strange fire

Repeat Three Times

Exuberance

Book of Leviticus 9:1 – 11:47

Torah reading: ***Shemini / Eighth***

On the day their father is inaugurated as High Priest, Aaron's sons, Nadav and Avihu, awash in youthful exuberance, trespass beyond the boundaries of required behavior and bring an unusual offering to the newly completed Sanctuary.

Reflection

You have stayed long enough at this mountain,
look back on your life and see where you have been.
Appreciate the wisdom gained thus far
through the hard lessons of life experience.
No one could have taught you
all you've learned and understood.
You have been shaped by your defeats
and by your successes.
Cherish the journey you are on,
choose what really matters most to you.
Move on from this moment
with resolve in your heart
to make each day a blessing,
a gift to yourself and those
whose life paths you cross.
You are not alone,
a loving caring Presence
Is walking right beside you.

Amen

You have stayed long enough
at this mountain

(Deuteronomy 1:6)

Breath Meditation for REFLECTION

This breath meditation invites you
to reflect on your life and then move on.

You have stayed long enough
at this mountain

(Deuteronomy 1:6)

Focus and breathe in:
You have stayed long enough

Focus and breathe out:
at this mountain

Repeat Three Times

Reflection

Book of Deuteronomy 1:1 – 3:22

Torah reading: ***Devarim / Words***

In view of the promised land, Moses speaks to the people for the last time. In this first of three long talks, Moses reviews their forty-year journey from Mount Sinai until the present moment. Moses seeks to bolster the people's spirits, for they will go on without him.

GRATITUDE

When you are filled with gratitude
acknowledge the abundance in your life with thanks.
Appreciate all the silent angels
who made this moment of gratitude possible.
Honor those who came before you,
who endured and thrived,
or maybe only survived.
Bring your awareness to the small sacrifices
and sheer good luck
that makes it possible for your heart
to overflow with generosity and thanks.
As you remember the gifts in your life,
hold on, no matter what,
so that every step on your journey
will bring you closer to dreams realized
and promises kept.

Amen

When you have eaten your fill,
give thanks

(Deuteronomy 8:10)

Breath Meditation for
Gratitude

This breath meditation calls you
to focus on gratitude for the blessings in your life.

When you have eaten your fill,
give thanks

(Deuteronomy 8:10)

Focus and breathe in:
When you have eaten your fill

Focus and breathe out:
give thanks

Repeat Three Times

Gratitude

Book of Deuteronomy 7:12 – 11:25

Torah reading: ***Eikev / If***

Moses reminds the people that they must always remember the source of all goodness and favor. He reminds them that God forgave them after the golden calf episode and gave Moses a second set of tablets.

Compassion

Keep your hand open
and your heart will open as well.
You will really see how to be holy in this world.
We are all needy and poor
at moments in our lives
alone and frightened,
discouraged and filled with despair.
Let yours be the hand that reaches out,
yours the heart that fills with compassion,
yours the eyes that see the humanity
in a homeless man's defiant stare.
You are the source of holiness in this world,
and you are held in God's open hand.

Amen

Open your hand
to the poor and needy

(Deuteronomy 15:11)

Breath Meditation for
Compassion

This breath meditation
softens your heart in compassion.

Open your hand
to the poor and needy

(Deuteronomy 15:11)

Focus and breathe in:
Open your hand

Focus and breathe out:
to the poor and needy

Repeat Three Times

Compassion

Book of Deuteronomy 11:26- 16:17

Torah reading: *Re'ei / See*

This week Moses reminds the people of our responsibilities toward the less fortunate, the poor, the shattered in spirit.

Patience

Do not judge yourself too harshly,
temper your inner judging voice
with patience and compassion.
Discern the voice of your own intuitive wisdom
and do what is right and good.
Be slow to judge others
and err on the side of kindness.
Allow your prejudices to be exposed,
upset complacency and desert inertia,
rather examine which voices speak truth.
Learn the patience of trees, protect and defend them
that you may sit in their shade
with none to make you afraid.
Trust that your inner sight is guided
by holy insight and Presence.
You will see clearly with a bright vision
Of who you really are.

Amen

Do what is right
in the sight of God

(Deuteronomy 21:9)

Breath Meditation for

Patience

This breath meditation strengthens your resolve to practice patience.

Do what is right
in the sight of God

(Deuteronomy 21:9)

Focus and breathe in:
Do what is right

Focus and breathe out:
in the sight of God

Repeat Three Times

Patience

Book of Deuteronomy 16:18 – 21:9

Torah reading: ***Shoftim / Judges***

Moses continues the second discourse, patiently instructing the people to pursue justice and guard against excesses.

JUDGMENT

May you be deliberate in judgment
and base your decisions on kindness.
Harsh judgment can be tempered,
this is the time to be slow
until bitterness and anger dissipate.
May you do the best you can right now
and trust that things will work out all right.
May you be blessed with clarity and discernment
and err on the side of generosity.
Allow your vulnerability to surface
as you calmly examine
which voices speak truth.
May you remember
from the deep storehouse of your soul
what it is like to be a stranger in a strange land,
so that your heart opens in compassion for yourself
and for all the world.

Amen

You know the stranger's heart,
for you were a stranger in Egypt.

(Exodus 23:9)

Breath Meditation for JUDGMENT

This breath meditation encourages you
to be less judgmental and more empathic.

You know the stranger's heart,
for you were a stranger in Egypt

(Exodus 23:9)

Focus and breathe in:
You know the stranger's heart,

Focus and breathe out:
for you were a stranger in Egypt

Repeat Three Times

Judgment

Book of Exodus 21:1 – 24:18

Torah reading: ***Mishpatim / Judgments***

The people, standing at the bottom of Mount Sinai, wait for Moses to return to them. He comes down the mountain, repeats the ritual and ethical laws God revealed to him and asks for their agreement. They proclaim their assent, and Moses goes back up the mountain to receive the stone tablets.

Courage

May you leave behind
all the stories that echo in your mind
and go forward to realize the unique mission
of your own precious life.
May you feel strong and courageous
as you travel to fulfill
the purpose of your creation.
May you awake to your potential,
and honor the core truth of your soul
even if it feels inconvenient or impossible.
May you be a source of courage
to all you meet on life's journey.
May you face your fears
And know you have what it takes
to vanquish them.

Amen

Be strong and courageous,
do not fear

(Deuteronomy 31:6)

Breath Meditation for
Courage

This breath meditation urges you
to trust your ability to conquer fear.

Be strong and courageous,
do not fear

(Deuteronomy 31:6)

Focus and breathe in:
Be strong and courageous,

Focus and breathe out:
do not fear

Repeat Three Times

Courage

Book of Deuteronomy 31:1 – 31:30

Torah reading: ***Vayelekh / And He Went***

As Moses considers his approaching death, he recites a poem to the people to bear witness to their fate and ultimate redemption. He assures them that they will thrive but they must be strong and have courage.

Loss

He proceeded to mourn for her
and cry out for her

(Genesis 23:2)

Loss

May you be blessed with long life
and the courage to enter the cave
where your ancestors rest.
May their memory inspire and sustain you
and bring you back
to the knowledge of who you are.
May you find the strength to walk
into the brokenness of your own heart
allowing that dear space to open.
May you receive the support
and comfort you need
as you are held in healing embrace.

Amen

He proceeded to mourn for her
And to cry out for her

(Genesis 23:2)

Breath Meditation for

Loss

This breath meditation honors feelings of loss
and the intention to enter the cave of your family's past.

He proceeded to mourn for her
and to cry out for her

(Genesis 23:2)

Focus and breathe in:
He proceeded to mourn for her

Focus and breathe out:
and to cry out for her

Repeat Three Times

Loss

Book of Genesis 23:1 – 25:18

Torah reading: *Hayye Sarah / Sarah's Life*

After Sarah dies, Abraham channels his grief and focuses on her memory. He manages to buy an appropriate burial site (a cave) to honor her.

The End of Life

May your spiritual essence journey on
with those who come after you
just as you bear the qualities of
those who came before you.
May your struggles to find favor in others' eyes
result in great inner and outer success.
May you be blessed to be surrounded
by family and loved ones
at the end of your life
even if they are only present in your memory
as was Jacob our ancestor.
May you pass on the legacy
of all you hold to be good and true
with steadfast unfailing kindness.

Amen

If I have found favor in your eyes,
act towards me with
steadfast kindness

(Genesis 47:29)

Breath Meditation at
The End of Life

This breath meditation invites you
to share your values with those who come after you.

If I have found favor in your eyes,
act towards me with steadfast kindness

(Genesis 47:29)

Focus and breathe in:
If I have found favor in your eyes

Focus and breathe out:
act towards me with steadfast kindness

Repeat Three Times

End of Life

Book of Genesis 47:28 – 50:26

Torah reading: *Vayekhi / And He Lived*

The book of Genesis concludes the saga of our ancestors: Sarah and Abraham, Rebecca and Isaac, Leah, Rachel and Jacob with Jacob's death. Jacob reviews his life and offers final blessings to his twelve sons from his deathbed.

Grief

May you find strength to move on
after the death of a loved one.
May you trust that love endures
stronger than death
and despite the loss and pain
so will you.
You will find a way
unknown now even to you
to release yourself
from guilt, regret and remorse
as the High Priest cleansed,
purged and offered a scapegoat
as an escape from excessive grief.
You will separate yourself
from death and from despair
and move forward slowly
one step at a time
so that you can find a way back
from the wilderness
to life in this world.

Amen

He shall send a scapegoat off,
into the wilderness

(Leviticus 16:10)

Breath Meditation for GRIEF

This breath meditation supports you in times of grief.

He shall send a scapegoat off, into the wilderness

(Leviticus 16:10)

Focus and breathe in:
He shall send a scapegoat off

Focus and breathe out:
into the wilderness

Repeat Three Times

Grief

Book of Leviticus 16:1 – 18:30

Torah reading: *Akharay Mot / After the Death*

Aaron, the High Priest, weighed down by grief at the recent loss of two of his sons, performs an atonement ritual. To assuage his grief, he makes expiation for his wrongdoings and those of his community and sends a scapegoat, bearing everyone's sins, off into the wilderness of Azazel.

Acceptance

May you accept that you cannot always choose
the circumstances of your life.
May you feel a measure of peace
in the face of life's terrors and dark moments.
Never cease to celebrate the freedom
to choose your own best path
to respond rather than react
to situations you cannot change.
Pain and loss will happen
but suffering can be lessened
by the way you respond.
Hold yourself gently in an embrace
of compassionate acceptance
each night as you lie down.

Amen

And you will lie down
with none to cause you terror

(Leviticus 26:6)

Breath Meditation for
Acceptance

This breath meditation comforts you
by trusting your response to terrors you cannot change.

And you will lie down

with none to cause you terror

(Leviticus 26:6)

Focus and breathe in:
And you will lie down

Focus and breathe out:
with none to cause you terror

Repeat Three Times

Acceptance

The Book of Leviticus 26:3 – 27:34

Torah reading: ***Bekhukotai / By My Rules***

Leviticus concluded with a promise and a threat. If the people obey God's laws, peace and prosperity will result; if Israel fails, disaster will follow.

LETTING GO

May you find comfort in the power of love
to pierce even the final threshold.
Even as you stumble and fall
you will rise upright strong and true.
May you listen to the inner voice
helping you find your footing.
May your inner awareness help you
transform difficult moments
into overflowing blessings
that nurture and sustain you.
Know you are not alone.
You share the miracle of being human
comforted by the shared companionship
of those who have suffered and lost.
Love is as strong as death
you see it with your own eyes.
And this is the blessing.

Amen

Love is as strong as death,
see it with your own eyes

(Song of Songs 8:6,
Deuteronomy 34:4)

Breath Meditation for
Letting Go

This breath meditation helps you find comfort and heal from loss.

Love is as strong as death,
see it with your own eyes

(Song of Songs 8:6, Deuteronomy 34:4)

Focus and breathe in:
Love is as strong as death,

Focus and breathe out:
see it with your own eyes

Repeat Three Times

Letting Go

Book of Deuteronomy 33:1 – 34:12

Torah reading:
Vezot Habrakha / And this is the Blessing

Moses will die alone by the kiss of God. No one will ever know where he is buried. Just before his death, Moses blesses each tribe with a farewell song.

Death Is Always Personal

Death is always personal.
We filter our pain through the memories of loss
felt and held in the recesses of our hearts
and the fiber of our beings.
As tears beget tears,
and sighs birth shuddering sighs,
we make meaning of tragedy and loss
in small and personal ways.
Death is always personal.
And the personal is our reality,
what we know to be real and true.
Each of us has our own precious memories,
the look of a loving smile, scent of sweet perfume,
taste of shared pleasure, feel of an all-enveloping hug,
sound of a well-remembered laugh.
Death is always personal.

Our personal losses do not isolate us,
we share the miracle of being human
comforted by the shared companionship of those around us.
When we open our hearts to our own personal memories,
we are embraced by community,
the community of all those who have suffered and lost.
One shared sigh, one common cry, one rhythm of release.
Communal yearnings link us to each other,
common dreams and connected longings recognize
our shared humanity.
We are all one – in our pain, in our grief,
in our tender suffering.
We can take solace and support from the presence of others,
the comfort and compassion of living in community,
acknowledging death is always personal.

Amen

Blessings for Weekly Torah Portions

According to over two thousand years of Jewish tradition, a specific portion of the Torah is read each week, beginning with the first book, Genesis, and continuing through Exodus, Leviticus, Numbers, and Deuteronomy. You can follow this order to create a weekly spiritual practice. It would be helpful to have your own Bible. You can use any bible, but I recommend the JPS Tanakh (Jewish Publication Society) because it divides the Torah portions into clear weekly readings.

Before you turn to the specific blessing for the week, it is very helpful to read the Torah portion for that week. Starting on Saturday afternoon is traditional, but you can choose any time for your practice that works for you. You can start a weekly practice anytime – you do not need to use a calendar. Following this weekly practice will lead you to read the entire Torah and to appreciate the narrative flow of this amazing work of sacred literature.

Genesis Blessings

		PAGE
Week 1.	Clarity - Bereshit	186
Week 2.	Trust - Noah	144
Week 3.	Inner Awareness -- Lekh Lekha	2
Week 4.	Angels - Vayera	148
Week 5.	Loss - Hayye Sarah	220
Week 6.	Family Relationships - Toldot	92
Week 7.	Leave - Vayetze	22
Week 8.	Struggle - Vayishlakh	96
Week 9.	Create a Family - Vayeshev	26
Week 10.	Family Tension - Miketz	100
Week 11.	Reconcile - Vayigash	104
Week 12.	End of Life - Vayekhi	224

Exodus Blessings

		PAGE
Week 13.	Possibilities - Shemot	14
Week 14.	Transformation - Va-era	18
Week 15.	Freedom - Bo	108
Week 16.	Rebirth - Beshallakh	10
Week 17.	Revelation - Yitro	36
Week 18.	Judgment - Mishpatim	210
Week 19.	Loneliness - Terumah	152
Week 20.	Perseverance - Tetzaveh	40
Week 21.	Stand Up - Ki Tissa	112
Week 22.	Rest - Vayakhel	44
Week 23.	Integrity - Pekuday	48

Leviticus Blessings

		PAGE
Week 24.	Balance – Vayikra	52
Week 25.	Warmth – Tzav	156
Week 26.	Exuberance – Shemini	190
Week 27.	Birth – Tazria	6
Week 28.	Cleansing – Metzora	56
Week 30.	Grief – Akharay Mot	228
Week 31.	Wholeness – Kedoshim	178
Week 32.	Imperfection – Emor	60
Week 33.	Simplify – Behar	64
Week 34.	Acceptance – Bekhukotai	232

Numbers Blessings

		PAGE
Week 35.	Resistance – Bamidbar	116
Week 36.	Protection – Naso	160
Week 37.	Heavy Burdens – Beha'alotekha	120
Week 38.	Doubt – Shelakh Lekha	124
Week 39.	Challenges – Korakh	128
Week 40.	Mistakes – Khukat	164
Week 41.	Intuition – Balak	182
Week 42.	Justice – Pinkhas	132
Week 43.	Promises – Mattot	68
Week 44.	Journeys – Massei	30

Deuteronomy Blessings

		PAGE
Week 45.	Reflection - Devarim	194
Week 46	Feeling Loved - Va'etkhannan	168
Week 47.	Gratitude - Eikev	198
Week 48.	Compassion - Re'ei	202
Week 49.	Patience - Shoftim	206
Week 50.	Release - Ki Taytze	136
Week 51.	Contentment - Ki Tavo	172
Week 52.	Empowerment - Nitzavim	72
Week 53.	Courage - Vayelekh	214
Week 54.	Listening - Ha'azinu	76
Week 55.	Letting Go - Vezot Habrakha	236

Acknowledgments

This book was dreamed and shaped with the committed and insightful help of the wonderful persistence of the Book Committee Chair Linda Schibel. The clear editorial insights of Marilyn Elias were invaluable. I cannot thank enough the following wonderful guides and friends: Marlene Canter, Jacquie Israel, Mary Rapoport, Julie Silver, and Rosanne Ziering! Each added unique insight and support.

My wonderful publisher, Judy Joseph and graphic designer Scott Johnson.

My deepest thanks goes to the wise suggestions of my rabbi sisters – Rabbi Toba August, Rabbi Karen Fox, and Rabbi Judith Halevy. And of course, my dear friend, Rabbi Steven Carr Reuben.

Stories truly take on a life of their own and I have told "The Curse of Blessings" (retitled "A Blessing Story" in this book) by Rabbi Mitch Chefetz over the years.

I am so very grateful for the suggestions of Natalie Caine and Nancy Shapiro. I thank the support of my extended family – Leslie, Jordan, Bari, Amy, Lance, and Samantha.

I was inspired to create this book because of all the people to whom I sent these blessings over the past five years and who keep asking for more (especially my mother).

I appreciate the insight and suggestions of fellow travelers, Carolyn Roberts and Elizabeth Nordquist.

Finally, this book could not have been completed without my beloved partner, Bob Auerbach.

RABBI SHERYL LEWART

Sheryl Lewart was a spiritual teacher who lectured and led workshops and seminars in Mystical Judaism (Kabbalah, Hasidism, and Mussar). She served as rabbi of Kehillat Israel, the largest Reconstructionist congregation in the world, serving more than one thousand families, in Pacific Palisades, California.

After graduating from Cornell University with a Bachelor of Science degree in child development and family relationships, she taught school in a rural Mennonite community near Philadelphia while studying for her master's degree in education at Lehigh University.

As an entrepreneur, she owned both an antiques business and a custom rug weaving business near New Hope, Pennsylvania, before her rabbinical studies at the Reconstructionist Rabbinical College (RRC) in Philadelphia. As part of her study she lived in Jerusalem while attending Hebrew University, and she was ordained at RRC in 1994, graduating with a Masters of Hebrew Letters.

She was a founding rabbinic cohort of the Institute for Jewish Spirituality, which is dedicated to exploring, renewing, and applying the abundance of Jewish spiritual traditions in order to enhance the inner lives of Jews and ultimately link the search for inner wholeness with social and environmental activism. She was also a member of Spiritual Directors International, whose calling it is to support and encourage holiness around the world and across spiritual traditions.

Having studied Spiritual Formation at the Mercy Center in Burlingame, California, Sheryl offered spiritual direction and guidance to help others understand that by developing our own spirituality we discover a deeper intimacy with God and a genuine compassion for all of creation. God, it has been suggested, is the wind that drives our ship, but it is up to us to turn the rudder and shift the sails in order to more fully catch the wind that freely blows.

In addition to her many other activities, Sheryl was an adjunct faculty member of the Reconstructionist Rabbinical College, was editor of *Jewish, Alive & American*, an innovative introduction to Judaism and conversion course in national distribution, wrote a column for the *Philadelphia Jewish Exponent*, and has been published in *Reconstructionism Today* and the *Los Angeles Jewish Journal*. She is the author of *Change Happens: Owning the Jewish Holidays in a Reconstructionist Tradition*.

She was a mother and grandmother and lived with her husband, Bob, in Los Angeles, California.

She completed the final draft of this book in the last weeks of her life. Rabbi Sheryl Lewart passed away on November 30, 2012. *Blessings for Life's Journey* is her Legacy.

Psalm 23

An Interpretation

Rabbi Sheryl Lewart

Holy One,
You care for me, I am content.

You lead me to still waters,
places of rest and renewal.

You guide me down the right path
to live a good life.

When I walk through a valley of deepest darkness
I feel no harm,
for you are with me.

Signs of your nearness
offer me support and comfort.

When faced with fear,
your love flows over me
and sustains me.

As I journey on, loving kindness finds me
each day of my life,
I come home to you.